Spring H...

poems by

Keith (KP) Liles

Plain View Press
P. O. 42255
Austin, TX 78704

plainviewpress.net
sb@plainviewpress.net
1-512-441-2452

Cover art, *Awakening*, by Dennis Lind (DennisLind.com), photographed by Eric Teela.

Photograph of author by Molly DeKruif (theblinkofaneye.com).

Acknowledgements

Many thanks to the publications in which the poems below previously appeared, sometimes in slightly different forms: *Anchorage Daily News*: "Dawn at the Confluence of the Kenai and the Russian;" *ICE-FLOE*: "Three Poems for the Autumn Equinox" and "4th and D;" *Fight These Bastards*: "Brothers in Rockford" and "O Largest Retailer;" *HazMat Review*: "Who Will Pay the Tab?" and "Morale Boost;" *insurgent49*: "Compassionate Care;" *Limestone*: "Reclaim"

Thanks also to Alaska Public Radio and the weekend show, <u>AK</u>, for broadcasting "Hard Core," "Love Junk (Testimony from a Congressional Hearing)," "Variations on E=mc^2," "Uninsured," "The Way of the Moose," and "P.I.C."

For the generous financial support that made this book possible, I thank the Rasmuson Foundation.

I am forever grateful to Deb Seaton and George Gee for all the nights onstage at Side St. Expresso — where I learned to trust the Muse.

for Matt Frank, John Huddle,
Tom Begich, and Catherine Curtis

For Diana —

Here's to mutual success
at AWP.

Chicago 2009

Keith KP Liles

Contents

Sane Craziness

Alaska Suite

Love

Civics

                              Sat down
under an umbrella and looked to see, among the diners
feasting, quarreling about their riven country,
if you were supposed to eat the bones. You were. I did.

—Robert Hass, "Regalia for a Black Hat Dancer"

Sane Craziness

If You Have Never

If you have never savored coffee before,
coffee is excellent here.
This is the place to taste.

If you've never considered flavor,
the coffee is chocolaty
and steams tropic earth.

If you've never cried at a funeral
or at least one truly heartbreaking film,
the coffee is pleasingly bitter.

Never allowed yourself a work-break,
a selfish gift, or the kids a time-out?
The coffee has unlimited refills.

If you've never delighted in
a mirror's reflection, everything
looks beautiful in daily-polished spoons.

If you've never escaped the neighborhood's
miseries: war, disease, hunger, poverty,
coffee is served with cream and sugar.

If you've never fused with love
—suffered its absence, its loss—
there's a spicy rich Turkish coffee.

Coffee's a double-espresso if
you've lost the intensity
of youth.

If you've never achieved balance
in the light and dark shades of your self,
the coffee is an Italian cappuccino.

And if you have never been scalded by coffee,
this is the place—and now is the time—
to taste. Coffee is excellent here.

Brothers In Rockford

And summer afternoons we'd laze at Grandma's.
Still in our Sunday bests, adolescent, sleepy
from waking early, bored by the pastor's sermon.
Sprawled across the mangy, straw colored carpet.
And the air thick with lilacs, lime scented talcum,
brown beans baking in the oven. And sun bored through the drapes.
And we'd lie in the heat, young beasts of the Serengeti,
swatting at the occasional fly, nudging the fan
in our favor, swiping at each other with the other paw.
If the Cubs were playing, the game would be on TV,
heat waves steaming from the mound, announcers babbling.
Once in a while the crowd might cheer
like a flock of startled birds—
the cameraman lingering on a bikini top—
and our bodies might remind us that we hadn't eaten yet, until
sleep, like the one true prayer, bowed our heads again.
And Dad and Grandpa hunched over the cribbage board
all day, like the first apes trying to get inside the ant hill,
sometimes grunting when the other mentioned words
like *Chernobyl, Libya,* or *AIDS.*
Mom talked to her mom about who'd *passed on* back in Missouri,
which uncle's farm was *going under* that week.
And she'd come into the room, to get out of the hot kitchen,
sit on the piano bench, where Grandma sang and played hymns
before arthritis made her joints ache *like a creek with no water.*
And Mom'd wonder aloud why we didn't go outside and
play. As if we didn't know what misery
we were prey to out there—hadn't already learned
the God we worshipped viewed our participation in this world
as a request for pain. As if the lush, fresh grass smell
blasting through the screen door, as the neighbor's mower
roared nearer, ever fooled us
into forgetting.

O Largest Retailer

What if the urge to shop at Wal-Mart

replaced hunger? Instead of meat and potatoes,
we craved a garden hose, pillow cases,
and a handgun—skipped breakfast

for clearance sales on aisle six, quick-pics
and a Sponge Bob flick—let the fruit rot?
Veggies be nixed! Of course there'd be

the hard-to-convince few who'd stay hungry,
who'd scrounge up the dough and take
their dream trips to Vanuatu, but who'd pay

out the whazoo or risk poisoning
for local fish
if offered Micky D's and a sunset stroll

down Flowers & Gifts?
Let's face it: we sit down at the table to talk
cheap shoes, reasonable cosmetics, a selection

of wristwatches at digestible price.
We've already been disencumbered
of so much! No more profane lyrics,

deprecatory literature, or going separate places
for prescription glasses, Viagra,
and bottled water. No more

suffering romance thanks to Singles Night
cart station liaisons. Would it be too much to ask
for a rollback on hunger as well?

Who can afford an appetite these days?
O largest retailer, gracious employer, skyline
painter, parking provider, nation greeter, economy healer—

hear your customers, your children.
Starve us, please! Help us feast on only
American wealth.

Hunch

More and more I see them
dipped, shrugged and rasp-gasping,
rolled newspapers clenched and
crushed. Bobble-heads, quasi-
humans. What monstrous punc-
tuation mutilates
their bodies's language?
A Tilde the Hunch!

some other ideas

too much television?
a lousy sucker punch?
meth, crystal prison?
A poisoned lunch!

      munch, munch—
maybe molars bite bite
down each shoulder?
      A new
brain leavens in their backs?
This one doing all the
thinking, all the voting?

some others' ideas

lifestyle, choice, the lazy
malady. The sculptor
dropped his trowel. Spawned out
crooked fishes stinking up
pristine communities.

But I too have a hunch

the family-breaking
robbing plotting gnarling
need-deforming grief
machine: poverty.

   Crunch, Crunch, Crunch

something fat on gravel
this way comes.
        GEORGIE!
Why if it isn't Dick
and Rummy's cat, always
eager for an extra snack.
Come 'ere smirky kitty.
Today I'm going to
feed you some of my lunch.

munch, munch, munch, munch

Spring Hunger

Gut-stunned.
Pain: a gun
marshaling eyes
beyond

the socket pale.
O, broken world,
you are a plateful
of embers in a mouth

drier than a fire-
well. Ache
wears me like a lover;
shudder, her kiss,

insists *keep
singing and eat.
Gnaw the charred
hearts of men*

into dust. My body
answers: I will eat
by singing this song,
by singing our songs.

Throat ablaze—
lips spit,
crackle, as my tongue
spoons flame.

Money

You were once called Moon,
before the lies, before the theft
of your soulful "o."
The thief: Greed, black sheep in the House
of Need.

And to make certain
your remaining "o" would never
rise, never escape
the orbit of his libido,
he rammed

his knee into your
torso, beat, broke you—with "ey,"
branded you like a
donkey, the ass that would endure
his load.

It's no wonder why
the tides charge dumbly as if whipped,
why we're strapped, awestruck
under a silver spell.   Can we
wriggle

out? Launch ourselves free
then reface your screaming face? Find
a currency un-
marked, unbound by the lunacy
of Greed?

Couch Potato School

1.

Contests that humiliate
    and eliminate en route to
idolizing a new
    champion of business,
            romance, endurance,
the arts: *Reality TV.*

And *the late breaking story,*
Abu Ghraib,
scandal as a scandal
of abuse;
    replayed
and remade endlessly,
            the drama—
in which the one-man-government
murders on behalf
of some character offstage

like America—
shoots

death as *nonstop*
action. We know
    it's neither *news*
nor *entertainment* but
            we tune in, flinch gawk
cheer, condemn,
laugh anyway.

What compels us to
torture with a beer
from an easy chair?

2.

Freedom and Justice
—the pilot—
is exhilarating. Unforgettable,

Lady Liberty thrashing
back agitprop
with her whip
of history
and particulars.

Nonetheless,
on cushions,
popcorn kernels
and crumbs, our numb asses
stay riveted
to *DUMB* —
with each fistful of food,
eschewing
even a change of
station, as both cheeks
hear blood
screaming
in every vein: *An embolis*

is in the building.

Shame

You would have me believe
I am too young to understand.

You would have me believe the team lost
because of my rookie flesh.

You would have me assume Coach's practice drills
teach me love of the game.

You would have
me look up to and obey him.

You would have me fear
missing out on manly fun.

You would have me
believe I am the only one.

You would have me own
the guilt, the crime.

You would have me fear other kids, my parents—
my memory cower beneath you.

You would have me trust only silence.
You would have me safe only in silence.

And older, you would have me convinced
speaking out for myself,

for others—and empathy—
each is dishonorable.

You would have me forever believe your
lies that have raped this soul

but not
this conscience.

     —for Richard Hoffman

Hatred

I crashed into its well
  like a tiger
      through
the barbed branch-
  ceiling
      of a Burmese trap.

I escaped
  the deadly stakes,
      but
whatever scent, whatever prey,
  lit my senses,
      I lost

in the fire: fury. I growled
  myself deaf,
      scratched my claws
down to bloody stubs
  against its steep
      muddy walls,

ran my rage
  in so many circles around
      its mortar I ground
my intelligence and instinct
  into ash.
      Whoever

approaches me next, no matter
  what the intention—
      my release, my head
for a trophy, or to pacify me with
  the very object of
      my hunger—know:

nothing left prowls this pit
　　but the pure urge
　　　　to kill.

Come, step to the rim

　　of my prison. Tell yourself
　　　　　　you're not
out in the wild but at the zoo—
　　any moment
　　　　you'll find a placard

that will tame my name
　　and eating habits. Surely
　　　　the hole is too deep
to leap from. Surely thick glass
　　separates us. Surely you
　　　　　cannot be menaced

by the beast striped
　　with malice
　　　　and fear,
who passes idle hours
　　sharpening teeth on wrath-
　　　　blanched bone.

Mailbox

Could that be
        a sliver of white
envelope—a piano key of promise?

No. Sorry old instrument.
Ain't played nothin' in days.
No replies for my poems. No news

from Nate stationed in Oman.
Enough already.
Through how many bars can a man

stand to rest? As if an unemployment check,
a letter from Billy Collins, or
a past due notice doesn't matter.

Worthless calliope! When I was a teenage boy with a baseball bat
        in my hands
          But I am a man,
a jazz pianist lost

without his *Rattapallax* beats
or junk mail jives—
who can't find his groove in

diminuendo.
The whole joint is
jumpin' and a cat

needs his ivories
if he's got to make silence
swing.

Uninsured

Last night I slept through the lunar eclipse
and missed a blood orange moon ripen near dawn,
but didn't put two and two together—
that magnificent celestial event
and my well-cared-for car catching on fire—
until I remembered my cat dying
the day after I'd gone to bed early
instead of watching a meteor shower.
And it's more than a little alarming
to learn that the heavens have clearly
been sending me signs all along. My God,
I wondered, standing beside the scorched husk
of my Taurus, what else have I missed?
An aurora borealis pink slip?
A solar flare foretelling the end
of my marriage and Elizabeth's affair?
A supernova shout: Hey, idiot,
that pain in your chest is a heart attack!?
What if, in the way birds are cued
into earthquakes, I've been privy to disaster,
but last night I blew my last chance to wise up
and now I'm on my own, as star-chartless
helpless and clueless as the next dumb schmuck?
I wait in the darkness on the rooftop
long after the house lights of zodiac-
covered neighbors have flicked off, cursing
myself for not owning a telescope.
When a cold wind blows, my chest tightens.
I look up at that luminous bobber.
That's it, I say, show me my fate. I'm not
out here only to hear Good night, and good luck.

Hard Life: A Stone's Memoir

(The autobiography of a stone thrown into the ocean by a bitter jilted
lover only to be thrashed back ashore during a devastating tsunami
— dropped inside a tank's cannon by a valiant dying soldier and fired
into the water once again, where, motionless on the sea floor, no less
than five thousand Great White sharks and other deadly predators
swam directly overhead — afterward, seemingly entombed in the stern
of a split sunken ship, scooped up by treasure hunters in a handful
of priceless jewels, then discarded onto the beach that would soon
be sullied by an oil spill—and enshrined in a museum exhibit meant
to teach humans how to guard against repeating gross blunders, allay
sadness, and to heal.)

Two Readers' Responses
to *Hard Life: A Stone's Memoir*

What a piece of schist!

Rock for brains.

Loyalty

Best expressed in a dog, right?
   Obedient. Eager to fetch.
   So devout he holds his bowels
   until you've woken up.
   And, of course, when you return
   from work, he smiles, pants, wags his tail—
   rewards himself happiness
   because he knew, positively
   knew, you'd be back.

               Wrong. He'd aban-
don you in a woof-beat
   for the postman's leg, a
   bitch's ass, or a dung-nugget
   halfburied in snow.

No. Loyalty is more like
   scratching your dog behind his
   deaf ear, letting him lick your face
   after he's called the moon to supper.
   Maybe even insisting
   that he sleeps on your bed.

Forgive Me,

reader: I am so little
of what you would have me be.

We all fall short

Visionary reader, if I were Cézanne, I'd feed
your eye astonishing kumquats.

Perhaps with apprenticeship

If I were Mozart, silent reader,
I would suffuse your mysteries with wondrous sound.

How 'bout a whistled tune

If I were I.M. Pei, crest-fallen reader, I'd build a glorious entrance
to the galleries of your dreams.

A lamp above the doorway will do

Ailing reader. If I were Mother Teresa,
I'd ease your suffering and nurse your soul.

Really, what I need is a hot cup of tea

Victimized and voiceless reader, if I were Jeanne d'Arc, I would
sacrifice myself to your great cause.

You're over the top now

If I were Angelo Gaja, I'd float your joy
in the finest Italian wine.

That's more like it

If I were your Shackleton down-trodden beaten No.No.No.
   hopeless reader,
I'd save you from the brink with my shout "Go On!"

You must dispose of the melodrama

But I am the poet, me. My tools: my voice, black ink, white paper.
My only talent: to walk beside you

Please, no self-righteousness or self-pitying

from blank space into darkness
and from the darkness into light.

That was rather nice. Keep at it. Listen closer. Do better.

Up, Up, and Away

Walking past the movie marquee
I do a double take. Superman's back!
Last I heard he'd fallen from a horse
and was paralyzed, if I'm not mistaken,
dead. Thank God he's O.K.
It's too hard to make your way in the world when
childhood idols can't stop
speeding trains or creepy villains
let alone when a caped crusader
can't raise himself...
               I, for one,
sincerely hope Superman's return
will spin fashion around into
accepting the wearing of underwear
on the outside of our pants—
ever since Christopher Reeves
played Superman as half hunk, half
bumbling wimp,
Clark Kent, I've staked my confidence
in knowing that dweebiness
is a sure sign of latent
extraordinary powers.

We need our superheroes
to be part hopeless dork,
because until science catches up
with our imaginations
and special effects, until the day when
we're all skilled with light sabers and laser guns,
or we can mutate into blade-clawed creatures,
it's encouraging to think that the man
inside the phone booth might reach
the baby carriage rolling into traffic in time,

some one blowing really really hard
might put out the fire,
some one like our bird-brained brother
or sister—who flies her plane solo—might
swoop in and steal us from harm.

Variations on E=mc^2

Energy equals mercy times accelerating courage

Excellence equals minute
calibrations and corrections—calibrations
and corrections

Education equals
a man's compassion rising
into public action

Extinction equals mass consumption
devouring culture exponentially

Epiphany
equals the mind's capacity
expanding at the speed of light to another power

A lifetime of Employment.
The reward equal to?
mini cheeses squared

Ecstasy equals the moonshine contract
of two young lovers

Eloquenly saying *mea culpa*
again and again

Morning Riff

I don't
believe you can—with a straight face, or
by laughing me off—tell me that
A-Bee-Du-Dah-Dah-Dee-Dee-Zu-Zu
doesn't mean happiness.

I won't let you argue with
what my ear told me.
I won't let you argue with my ear

   that saw
my woman scrambledance eggs
to Count Basie's "Jumpin' at the Woodside"

   that heard
penguins prepare for their voyage
from the ice-shelf melting
just outside
my kitchen window

   that rinsed off
last night's wine, lovemaking,
by showerslurping coffee,
and cleaned room for more, more,
more.

A-Bee-Du-Dah-Dah-Dee-Dee-Zu-Zu—

Happiness.
How could it mean anything else? How else
could it sound?
Do you have another way to say it?
Go ahead,

let me hear

Alaska Suite

The Way Of the Moose

Close behind the grazing moose—because
he doesn't see? he flouts all danger? he doesn't know
one hoof-shot will open his head like a flicked
Zippo?—the cyclist speeds by. My eyes bulge
and the silent scream *Kick him!*
surges through muscle. With such violence I'm stunned.
                                        I breathe deep,
exhale, ask myself *Why am I so mad?*
After all, thousands of dangers
must threaten my life—visible
with perfect clarity to others—to which
I am oblivious or I ignore. *Samantha's kiss?*
Those third Maker's on the rocks reading before bed?
Bears on the Kenai when I fish after dark
to avoid hordes of daytime anglers:
                                        crowds of morons—like
the biker, who'll remind me of my own
willingness to provoke fate
despite the dummies' history of battered skulls
and crippled psyches. Is the risk of death necessary
in order for us to learn?

The moose swivels its head, but doesn't skewer the cyclist.
Shows no sign of rage or alarm at the whirling machine,
the hominid snarling. Goes right on munching. Folds
its legs then rocks its massive cargo—stinking
of marsh, heat, rot—
down into the bay of grass with such grace
I am chastened.

At a safe distance, avoiding direct eye contact,
I walk by, telling myself *look at ease.* And bow
for its gross gentility, to give my respect
to the beast I name: teacher.

Dawn At the Confluence Of the Kenai and the Russian

After I've brought in a sockeye salmon. All right,
after I've muscled a
fish out of the water and
dragged it across the bank,
I hold it. I pin it down
and pray: "Thank you for gracing me
with this catch. May I be worthy.
Bless this fish—its spirit—for its life sacrificed for
my hunger, my sport."

I suppose I want to make it known—
(to whom? I'm not sure. God?
The animals? Hey, I haven't forgotten how
a bear mauled that poor bastard six hours ago
exactly where I'm standing now)—or maybe I need
to remind myself—that I am
grateful, not just some flippant jerk
participating in this ancient,
animal act—maybe I'm hoping to save my ass—
maybe I'm not ready to deal
with what it tells me about myself
that I feel giddy, exhilarated, as I'm about to clobber
a Red lifeless with my bat—
because sometimes I wonder if
my rituals protect me or

keep me from knowledge. You see,
sometimes—though fish are supposedly too dumb
to feel pain—when a salmon slaps,
head then tail, head then tail, across the rocks;
when I look into that dilated, marbled eye;
and when its body shudders after the first blow
the only word for
        The only word is horror.

40

And other times, I'd swear—with its
upturned chin and opened mouth—I'd swear
it's smiling, like it's in on a joke—it's seen
the larger creature behind my back
and is satisfied with the story—

that when you're ripped from the world
you've always known, you're
hauled off into an excruciating,
exquisite, new light.
As if the salmon's found religion, or has
always enacted it—forecast and swum to
the violent end—
or somehow perceives my faith
better than I ever will.

I mean, it has to go one way or the other.
It can't be both, right? The dead fish is either
yukking it up, ecstatic—has discovered that
its antics while thrashing to escape my hook
only kept it in the stupid current, delayed
its paradise run—or
its whatever you want to call it   soul
is no more than bludgeoned brain bits.
I'm either a brutal caveman
who should shelve his gear and join PETA
or I'm a hands-on gourmand
who earns his supper.

Who can say what the truth is
in a fish's face? It's not going to tell you
and if anything else intends to impart knowledge
so far all I see is that I'm an idiot
for worrying the afterlife of dinner.
Or I'm not—that meat
is sweet once it's on the table.

Waiting Outside At the Downtown
Transit Center In January

Almost 9 a.m.   the sky a sneer of cobalt blue
along the horizon   half of us wear sunglasses
to shield our eyes from the wind—blowing so hard it snaps us in and
    out of buses like a tango
partner dancing to prove his manliness   Feels like being on a
        spider
web—shoulders scrunched in cold, cocooned—as we smoke   you
        know the need is something awful
to stick it out in this shit   And for what? School? Shakespeare?

Should've taken my slope money—screw Shakespeare—
gone someplace hot like Mexico or Argentina   Yeah, shaken off
        these winter blues
roaming the Pampas, Patagonia   strutted into Buenos Aires all full
of Spanish, criolla and asado, humidity   drop my sunglasses
for passing mujeres   Hell, I'd even let those—what do you call
        those spiders—
tarantulas—I'd let tarantulas crawl on my chest I'd be so laid back
        Tango

every night until my ass dropped   Spend the days working on my
        tan   Go
find myself an orchard where the wind shakes pears
mangoes bananas from the trees   fruit for everyone—spiders
campesinos, me and a señorita filling a powder blue
dress that would erase my picture of #2's map-curves   sunglasses
pinning back her black hair longer than the Alaskan nights and
        their awful

dark mornings   Ah, who am I kidding?   I'd get the most awful
sunburn of my whole damn life   my tango'd
turn me into the next William Hung   sunglasses
never sit right on my nose   and the truth is I need to hear
        Shakespeare—

hear more of those "bare ruined choirs"   fuck the guys and their
          jokes—roses are red violets are blue
I'll never go back to Prudhoe Bay   Argentina?   Some tropic
          spider

would bite me my first ten seconds off the plane and I'd die
          babbling, "spider
antidote, por favor."   Aw hell, here comes old Beatrice looking for
          a smoke.   "Hey Doug, got a cigarette?   This is
          the most awful
cold I've ever lived through. I can't feel a thing.
          My tits are blue."
"Here you go" I laugh and hand her two sticks, wonder what's wrong
          with me—we're half frozen and I'm dreaming
          about the tango.
Who am I to escape this place?   Beatrice ever have someone dance
          with her, have Shakespeare
recited to her? She ever get a lazy day in the sun—glasses

of cold beer on a table between her and her man? Naa, I've seen the
          bruises under her sunglasses,
seen the eyes bloodshot sleepless   eyes that slide down their drains
          like spiders
at anyone's—anyone's—look   eyes overworked, scabbed from
          tears, scared and lonely   that have never had a
          Shakespeare
compare her to a summer's day, never glimpsed a way out of her
          awful
mess—the custom-fit mess that each one of us is handed to tango
with until the music stops or   DAMN, wind about blew

#60 onto the sidewalk   All I know is that when I get out of this
          fucking cold and I take off these sunglasses I mean to let
          everyone see all the good, all the awful
fantasies I've ever carried   no spiders in these eyes   no, sir.
          Here's my bus.   Brutal tango
never counted on this blue collar ass sitting down for Shakespeare.

Wait Service, Summer In Anchorage

1.

The gubernatorial hopeful gulps
    an oyster, sucks
    champagne through his teeth
as if whistling outside-in.
Smiles his glycerin smile.

"In my opinion, (the mouth
    answers its own question)
    absolutely, we see signs of
global warming and
to tell the truth—we love it!"

His slender neck dredges
    crouped laughter
    as his fist quakes
the butter dish and knife
off the table. I pick up

my good excuse to leave and earn
    the fat tip, return to
    the server's station, pour
syrah into a soup cup
and swallow fast.

2.

11:15 p.m.
Sunset. Mt. McKinley obscured
by smoke from Siberian
and homegrown wildfires. Waves claw
Shishmaref into the sea.
Men school in Ship Creek,
searching for a King, as our

distinguished guest—
who must know I avoid him
—sees a spectacular

endless twilight, a gas line,
and an ANWR drilled.

3.

Despite the news of tourists sickened
from bad, raw oysters—
too-warm-water—after a swig of soup,
I round the corner with his half-dozen.
And we stare at each other
as I set the dish in front of his neatly-folded hands—
neither of us flashing the slightest sign
of hope that the other will be poisoned
by what festers behind
pursed lips.

Who Will Pay the Tab?

Shitfaced at F Street Station,
    the Airman concentrates   on finishing
a draft. He's lived for this day—
    Elmendorf's news
of his deployment.

    His pregnant wife
prepped for this hardship, this Iraq.
    Still, he can't
rally   the words, can't fit
    the idea *of duty*
into the daily   order
    of family.

On CNN, President Bush
    stumps to privatize Social Security.
Across the ticker underneath guns
    the Administration's effort to
stop money aimed
    at Gulf War POWs. A pilot grumbles

I remember...Daddy
    promising...   *read*
my   *lips...*   The Airman
    tips back his last sip of beer,
struggles with jacket zippers,
    can't find his wallet.

This round's on me soldier.
    He looks up. Uncertain
if he's heard the bartender
    or the television.

Three Poems For the Autumn Equinox

Fireweed cotton
floating
in red wine.

Termination dust,
bowl of salt beside the range,
moose skull in moonlight.

the days go
quickly I go
in them

The Spill

—after Grace Paley

Here I am in the garden smoking,
a young man with shaky hands
and a face   flushed with shame.

How did this happen?
This isn't who I wanted to be—

Trained, a waiter,
taking orders from the governor—
foie gras and candied nuts—
apologizing as wine
slicks the table.
      Should've laughed,
said *progress—uncontrollably fluid,*
right?

Was it possible to stop the spread?
Prevent the collision?
That's my manager inside the window.
She's talking to the House Speaker,
dipping her blouse
as she pats stain with white cloths.

She's talking about the world's grand story
and so forth,   growth as oil
or timber. I tell my busboy
run over to our boss. Ask her
to stand beside me for a minute. I

am suddenly exhausted by my desire
to punch her lush, resourceful lips.

Handling Late Winter

Immense darkness,
pain-oblivious cold.

Give me coffee—black
and strong—in a thick,

white, ceramic cup
that retains heat

(No sugar)
and is safe to hold.

Love

Long, Painful, Break-up Recoveries
Have Been Done To Death

From Francie: snow pants
and ski boots. A wool
hand-knit scarf from Haidi,
socks galore
from Sister. Mittens from Mom...

Dumped by Danielle just
before Christmas, gifts
from female friends outfitted me,
suggested that I'd be

all right—that I might have fun—
if I stayed outdoors,
if I kept bundled-up
in the cold.

But since I've met you, Beth,
my legs sting
and steer me toward your house.
My fingers shiver and sweat under fleece.
My socks

slump down around my heels.
I tug continually at the fabric
chafing my throat. My clothes

want off.
They beg me: *hurry*
embrace her and allow
nothing to separate hot skins.
I can't get inside fast

enough.

Hard Core

"Pick one," the star of her culinary class,
Chef de Cuisine of the hottest new restaurant in town,
says to me, standing in front of the apple bins
at fall market.

Chalked on the overhead slate,
I read the options: Gala, Braeburn, Jonagold,
Granny Smith. Cameo? McIntosh?

As her waiter, I know I should ask *for dinner
or dessert? Golden or red?*
Not that her answer would help.

And she is watching,
weighing my intuition, judgment, compatibility,
or so it seems after three years single—
the woman who's still interested
watching me.
I grab a Fuji.

O, Lucky Day!
Symmetrical!
Broad, proud shoulders!
Most handsome apple.

"Naa. That one's bad," she says.
"Too perfect. Always buy scuffed produce.
Nature's beaten it up and given it flavor."

Her eyes scan exactly
where mine have just looked
and I see myself in her kitchen
where she makes decisions with knives.
"Here. This one," she says.

She holds out a gashed apple,
yellow-bald, lopsided.
I blush, hesitate.

Unsure if I'm cut for this love,
I climb the smooth wobbly
button-ladder of a chef's whites
to where I find a deeply-lined face,
eyes—fierce, bright blue,
inviting me,
saying, Come, reach out your hand, silly boy.
I deal exclusively in bruised flesh,
damaged fruit. I am the orchard keeper
here, where everything tastes better
with abiding wounds.

Love Junk

(Testimony from a Congressional Hearing)

Nothing will stone you higher
than love. Look around—you see
anything else that sends the
entire species searching for
a constant fix? Nothing's so
pure, so potent, as love. One
hit, one taste, and your head'll fill
with ecstasy—not some dull
hallucination, but every
breath a gift can't be hurt soar
through the day paradise.
Baddest dope around. The rush
takes hold instantly and lasts
for so long you can't remember
your life before
                    Dangerous?
Hell yeah it's dangerous.
People forget sleep and food,
trash pickup, rent, believing
they can live on love alone.
And I'm no liar—nothing
nothing ever hurts so bad
as coming down from love.
But try to live without it

What? Oh, you think we can pass
on risk and we'll be OK?
Right. Look, no matter how
wasted love may leave you
it'll never leave you empty.
I tell 'em all, if not
today, someday you will buy.
Did I come looking for you?

Better buy now before you're
so desperate you settle for
a lousy imitation
that'll rot your guts and dreams.
Buy here where the deal is clear
and the goods are clean. You know
a bargain when you see one.

Look me in the eyes. The price
of love is locked, equal
to its reward. Yeah, lemme
see into your many-pained eyes.

Pay up, partner—in this hustle
no one scores by stalling.

Friday Night Fun

Clarissa slides down the pole.
She stops, legs widespread, moneyed
thong thumping to AC/DC's
"You Shook Me All Night Long"
six inches above my face.
So I raise my buck high, chug
a Pudweiser fast—eyes closed—
because I hear that moral
son-of-a-bitch Keith Liles
speeding down the synapses
of reason and inquiry
like the outraged wife racing
'cross town to kick my ass good.

Can't I be a man for one
night, for urge, for skin, for porn,
for perfume, the thrill of sex
without cost—or the pain of failed
romantic maneuvers? For
Ben's bachelor party Christ's sake?
You realize Damn *Clarissa*
is someone's mother, spouse,
sister, daughter? Think of your
family onstage before
men behaving just like you.
Oh theregoesthetop. Waitress,
another beer please. *How can...*
Shut up. Shut up. These girls earn
a killing. And they've CHOSEN
this line of work. Look at those...
And whose dollar strokes their choice
into an attractive option?
Whose dollar remainders them
as objectified lust?

What's the harm in a little
                    excitement that will only
        benefit Debra later?
        You're so considerate, Keith.
Do you think these CEOs
        can't afford a fuck? You think
                the ratio of premature
                        ejaculations to
                satisfied girlfriends will throb
        in women's favor tonight?
"I'm going outside for air,"
        I scream at my guilt-deaf group
                even as a pair of panties
                        lassos Ben by the neck
                and lifts him into blissdom.

From here, the story I'd like
                    to tell would slump a stripper
        in the building's shadow
    like a crumpled tissue, hose
torn, snorting her tears—or
    stand her under the marquee,
                smoking, eager for her date.
                        Either one, seeing me, snaps
                "What the fuck you looking at?"
        so cold my testosterone
is censored permanently.
        Or better yet, it would thrust
                me back in for Bubble Gum's
                        lap-dance and bust my nut.
                But the truth insists I stomp
        to my car, pull out—seeing
  these girls. As their job: showgirls
    in a play with the all-time-
                world's-greatest opening act,
                        whose climax can't be screwed up

except by a jerk like me—
the lousy dog gone behind
the wizard's emerald curtain.

Swig from my flask. Springsteen cranked
above the volume of thought.
Home, out on the balcony:
couples streak through the hard rain
like pin balls, lighting up bars,
restaurants, movie theaters.
Bombed on a bottle of cheap
Aussie wine, I wait, watch
—such a dull game—hope for love's
lightning: a flash which might pack
the amps to strike me

In Search Of a Classic Life

After watching *Citizen Kane* on DVD,
certain I've missed the ingenious nuances
which bolster its acclaim as The greatest film,
I'm tempted to roll it again, this time with
running commentary by the experts, the passionate aficionados,
Peter Bogdanovich, or Roger Ebert.

But, as much as I'd like to learn
everything—production history, camera angles,
Welles' innovations, actors' feats of daring—
I remind myself that excessive explanation
kills joy; not to mention, some standards for perfection
we should know better than to let others set for ourselves.

Besides, I like to trust my own wits and to believe that
if I pay close attention, if I'm earnest about living better,
fuller, I'll get along okay, I won't miss or foul-up
too much. Or so I tell myself after a night's dream
in which I've watched my entire life
with commentary by the Spielbergs of holiness—Gandhi,

Martin Luther King Jr., God:
   Pride keeps you at arms length from your brothers and sisters Yes
   I know If you had cast violence from your heart
   you would not have slept in Julia's bed while with Stephanie
   Yeah I get it I know I'm sorry Pissing
   on Kyle's car door handle?   The world burns around you

   and you come to us as though your problems matter
I'm sorry I'm sorry I promise to do better
but, hey, look, sometimes even the best of us can't avoid
trouble, like the small plane in tip-top shape,
cruising along, until a mad duck zings into an engine. A scenario
in which no degree of integrity can save.

Can't the movie do all the talking?
Answer, justify, propose, sadden, delight, all by itself,
on its unflappable terms? Even when I shatter love
and the budget's too puny for another take?
Listen to yourself. (That insufferable commentator:
me) *You're doing it again. Don't
be afraid.* But I am. So I'm left pushing
for those moments when the voices should shut up
and let the screen play unbroken—like when Charles Foster Kane
rampages through the room of the wife who's just left him:
Orson vanishing into Kane, into the childish wounded bully:
silent: face contorted; the shot from the floor

horrifies; the story achieves electrifying tragedy—
and then, afterward, the character returns
to the actor observing himself acting. Changed
by the discovery of powers within him—good and bad.
And begins to marvel upon them. Until all that's left
is the desire to shoot the next scene.

  —for Allison

P.I.C.

My partner in crime, though not the princess
in charge as you would prefer I concede:
patience. I can't fall for you faster—
I adore each perfumed intimate card
and panic if the coat you gave me
goes missing, and will forever cherish
the framed pictures of us in Chicago
(not to mention the sight of your pants
in the ceiling fan), so don't be discouraged
because I haven't proposed inside your
calendar target. It is possible
I'll come to my senses as your parents
not so implicitly commanded
sooner than you think. Your love
teaches me quickly. Already, I've learned how passion
insists upon combustion, planning invites
chaos, and that pain is central to all
healthy couples. I promise to perform
intricate and infinite contortions
of compromise to remain in your good graces.
In prayer, I call you paradise itself.
Consider pardoning your idiot
companion. I pledge to interrogate
the concerns and police the illicit
cynicism that prohibit me from
initiating our permanent union.
What I'm trying to say is please,
I can't live without you, my partner in crime.

As Van Morrison's *Tupelo Honey* **Plays**

Bacon, saxophone, coffee, flutes.
Our first shared breakfast, you in
my clothes. Please, please, please, Terry,
as you confide your arch griefs—
the mother who's blamed you for her

decisions, who's never hidden
her wish for you unborn; the father
who split; the fling whose disease
fevers you; oh and there's more,
plenty more—forgive me

for laughing. I wield no words
to convince you of my hope,
to express my delight as I detect
my fear sentries' posts unmanned.
No alarms sounding. No cannons

loaded in the eyes' turrets.
No planes dropping leaflets (*Strike back
at noon! Rendezvous with Alex!*)
to ignite the mind's resistance.
Instead, fearlessness. How refreshing.

Amazing, this utter ease,
this instant reckless peace
I knew only as myth
until this morning, this song,
you crying. Until you.

What should I make of your smile?
A shield for your awakening horror?
Or is your disbelief
under siege by the exact
same fascination? Would you

agree if I said, "Forget
about opening your heart—
we can do that with our pets
—but unto me you must disgorge
your wounds?"

Scourge me with your pain,
smirch me with your fears, pelt me
with your hate hail
and curse me with your kiss.
I am the suture for this agony,

this healing, called love.

Dreams Of Manhood

If I'd ever listened to the pastor as a kid

I'd've known my wish was a double-dog-dare to God
to deform me as punishment for vanity, but
I was too busy praying "Dear Lord, please help me grow

thick hair and a big dick, so that I may grow up just like
the older boys. Maybe even a little better,
a little bigger—if it be thy will of course."

I was too busy dreading another humiliation,
like when Todd jumped over me on the basketball court
and came down on my head, shouting "Eat that

you little turd!" as I choked down the stench of his armpit,
and wiped his sweat from my face and hands. I
learned quickly that both strength and truth manifest in

the body; unless I had a Schwarzenegger physique
or Brad Pitt's looks, I would turn weak, unpopular, and—
if I didn't pray in earnest—into a HOMO.

Days? maybe inches? maybe friendships?
Love? The thinking about, the measuring,
cost me plenty. That prickhead Fear.

Maybe adulthood is knowing that the luxuriance
of my hair and the dimensions of my cock
never swayed a battle or a girl's affection.

I hear the pastor now: *Boys, it's stupid to not ask*
for directions when you're lost. If a man listens
to those who love him, especially the women

who love him, and himself, he will understand
that his mind and heart empower him beyond
his muscles or sex. Only love determines his shape.

I walk into the kitchen to get a round
of Bulls game beers for the guys. My sister sits at
the table with her high-school friends. They trade glances.

And I can almost smell Todd's sour pit again
when I hear one of the girls whisper "Your brother's cute.
Is he   big?" My head stashed in the

refrigerator, imagining that after the giggles stop
Annalise will say "What my brother keeps
in his pants he carries above his belt."

Civics

4th and D

—with a line from Langston Hughes

He slept like a rock or a man that's dead,
slept like a rock or a man left for dead.
"NO" he groaned when I tried to lift his head.

He held no covers in his cold hard bed,
held no covers in his cold civic bed.
No sadder place a man could've laid his head.

Mister, why don't I take you where you'll be fed?
Why don't I take you to where you'll be fed?
He growled "How 'bout a fifth you goddamned kid?"

So I bought him a thick blanket instead,
I bought him a thick blanket-fix instead.
Bought a blanket. Set it on him. And fled.

He sleeps in my mind like a man that's dead,
same as that blanket and the way I fled.

Reclaim

A young poet reads Robert Hass—"the gazelle's head turned; three
    jackals are eating his entrails and he/is watching."
    —and can't find his way to a poem.

He swears it's enough to enjoy eating and fucking
and spending money—those rewards are hard earned too.
Three days later he comes across the quote for the day
in the financial section of the local paper,
J.F.K. saying, "When power corrupts, poetry cleanses."

There is so much work he wants to see done.
But

Language, if on our payroll at all, has proven
erratic, has produced, at best, unreliable goods and many mangled
    limbs.
He has tried to tell two women now that he loves her with full force,
said "I love you" as an animal cry as an oath as a benediction, and
    this morning he woke up to shovel horse shit
    in exchange for room and board.

We're told *be careful what you ask for* and then we're told to
tell the nice man what you want. Is it any wonder we're so seldom
    satisfied in
our wanting?

Because he lives by words and mistrusts their assembly
he inhabits silence.

I hear my pulse. The blood throb music.
Not with or without objective. It is provocation—joy, curse, charge—
this radical

sound of weighing.

Compassionate Care

Relax. The abdominal discomfort
you are experiencing aboard the cruise ship
is not attributable to a viral outbreak
but a slight increase

in pathogen population. We suggest you quickly,
but calmly, privatize your Social Security account.
Both ingest and invest in Blubegonal. Not only
will you prevent your pancreas from putrefying but you *may* earn
a modest fortune.

A prescription of Blubegonal includes
an evening's entertainment, which features legitimately-wed
heterosexual performers; however, we advise against
discontinuing your membership in the NRA
or making contributions to Muslim affiliated charities
until Arab staff has been quarantined
and the hull resanitized.

Conservative estimates show
Blubegonal provides relief within minutes
for heartburn, nausea,
shock-jaw, propaganda sensitivity, Tourette's
and vexing class consciousness.
Immunity to all international law is immediate.
Still, please refrain from urinating in the ocean.

For best results, administer Blubegonal
along with quick-bake tanning lotions; our scientists
tell us unwarranted fears of UV-rays and global warming
have depleted the body of beneficial cancers
and precipitated the current health situation.

Permanent tax cuts; daily, standardized tests;
and destabilizing social programs in favor of military spending
are supplements to Blubegonal. Not cure-alls.

If symptoms such as divisiveness,
paranoia about the alleged encroachments
on civil liberties, or acute dread
of media consolidation persist, consult the captain

who also happens to be an Exxon recognized physician.
Blubegonal is not
for those with high tolerance.

Though no one besides you can claim ownership
of your own health, we makers of Blubegonal understand
we're all in this together, and feel
it is our patriotic mandate
to make your escape from democratic reality

as pleasant as possible. Stop by our kiosk now
(located between the naval recruitment office and ATM),
where our sales representatives are eager to get you
back on your feet in time to disembark on your next
third world shopping splurge and condo purchase. Why
prolong securing your future

when Blubegonal is here to help?
Stop stressing. Enjoy the trip.
Always wash your hands.

Blubegonal has received favorable opinions by the FDA, EPA,
and Department of Homeland Security. Side effects may include
slight bloating, memory loss, lightening of skin pigmentation,
male pattern baldness, and an infallible perception of righteousness.

The Citizen

Rich, poor
Irish, English, Protestant,
Catholic—
He fought beside, for
And against them all. His only allegiance:
Rhetoric. His only tactic:
Discourse. His only reason: justice.

Between his pen and his parliament, he
Risked his life defending revolution,
Inalienable rights, and the oppressed.
No one in the empire could purchase his mind or
Silence his tongue with the "dirty little traffic for
Lucre and
Emolument." Swift, Wilde, Joyce,
Yeats. Where is his name?

"Safely in his coffin, the process of transforming
Him into a colorful, fabulous, and
Essentially harmless genius could begin."
Remember *The School for Scandal?* Warren Hastings
Impeached after the Begum speech? By whom Frederick
Douglas learned to read? Because he dared
Articulate the truth he died in debt, drunk, alone. He
Never failed his duty to be free.

"10-31"

(Bridge Jumper)

No barrier splits the sea and the rail
on the other side of the Golden Gate,
The Chord, where the reasons *not to* fail.

Tourists snap shots, boats drift through their sail.
During that moment when the soul screams, "Wait!"
nothing obstructs the void between sea and rail.

Dead-straight ahead—the island, the jail:
gravestone of greed, cruelty, and hate—
when lovingkindness cannot fail.

How many jumpers cry behind fog's veil
as cost, aesthetic, and effectiveness debate
building a barrier between sea and rail?

Imagine: the walk from home, dropping a note in the mail—
"If one person smiles," you'll break the date—
arriving to The Chord without fail-safe—

inching, curling, contracting like a snail
on the other side of the Golden Gate
where nothing divides the sea and the rail,
where all reasons—all chords—fail.

Firsthand Knowledge

I drive by no ditch of decapitated countrymen
on my way to work. No orphaned child wandering
through a storm-ravaged city
tugs at my shirt. No closet of clothes
once owned by grandparents gassed at Auschwitz
haunts my hangar-thin frame. Disease-
free and nearly thirty—not a jumbled
joint in this jigsaw puzzle of muscle,
blood and bone. Yet there are nights when
the hurt of my neighbors and the silence of the people
wounds me so deeply I am certain that even the unfamiliar
world's news imprisons my spirit and threatens
my soul. Is pain the court I can testify in
only as an expert or eyewitness? Or, as a resident of Earth,
should I consider myself as being already under oath?
If I, we, swear in our lives to empathy, will the
anonymous injured win justice?

I know enough to allow a drink of clean water
to inform me about suffering
at even the farthest reaches of the globe. And compel me to act.
May my life be the enemy of ignorance and idleness,
my conscience a shield, my voice
a blade of healing.
Lebanon, Darfur, Katrina, Iraq—
as I read the paper each morning, I speak names aloud,
I arm my thirst.

    —August, 2006

Morale Boost

Each life intact. Each soul a single piece.
I pray each one
comes home from battle
unruined. My gratitude salutes
the men and women serving

in the armed forces of the United States.
That is why
I must say I do
not support our troops. I do not
support our troops. I say this

to bring them home. I say this because their
great sacrifices
we betray—their blood
spills in vain—if we cannot speak
freely. I say I do not

support our troops because I support them.
I say I do
not support our troops
because we forget how to listen
to what we don't want to hear.

Our inability to contend with
dissenting ideas
whittles our
attention-span into a toothpick—
carves our faculty of reason

down to the splinters of delight in
the familiar and
disdain for what is
not instantly agreeable.
I do not support our troops

because we grow deaf in the lack of speech.
I do not support
our troops because we
die from lack of speech. We are all
dying from lack of speech.

I do not support our troops because war
recruits more
terrorists than it
stymies. I do not support our troops
because I will not comply

with failed vision, disingenuous talk,
awful judgment:
the Fear Cabinet's
shoddy leadership. I do not
support our troops because God is

love—the laying down of weapons and hate.
I do not support
our troops because
the courage of mankind to refuse
killing for any idea,

any government, or paycheck will spark
the wildfire purge
of this world's dead-wood values
and ancient antagonisms.
I do not support our troops

because the history-hardened thirsty
heart of the world
we must flush clean of
its blood. With our greatest dream: peace.
With the old truth: as long as

we murder to solve our conflicts we are
not free, we will
never be free. We
are not free. I do not support
our troops because they cannot

set us free. I do not support our troops
because
I have faith
we will earn
our freedom.

—July 4th, 2005

—July 4th, 2005

Reconciliation

To all readers, all listeners,
for whom this book caused
either grief, shock,
confusion,
hatred, nausea,
or terrific boredom—
refer to the individuals
honored in the dedication.

Blame them.

About the Author

Keith (KP) Liles was born in 1976 in Woodstock, Illinois. He earned a BA in Rhetoric from the University of Illinois, Champaign-Urbana, and an MFA in poetry from the University of Alaska, Anchorage. After twenty-five years of promising his first book, he is happy to give friends and family reason to believe that he is only somewhat cracked.

Printed in the United States
130199LV00002B/286-339/P